MARY BERRY
Cooking at Home

MARY BERRY
Cooking at Home

THAMES MACDONALD

A Thames Macdonald Book

© Thames Macdonald 1983

First published in Great Britain in 1983
by Macdonald & Co (Publishers) Ltd
London & Sydney

 A member of BPCC plc

in association with
Thames Television Limited

ISBN 0 356 09742 0

Printed in Great Britain
by Blantyre Printing & Binding Ltd.,
London and Glasgow.

Editor: Julie Dufour

Design: Kathy Gummer

Jacket and Food Photography:
Rex Bamber

Production: John Moulder

Macdonald & Co (Publishers) Ltd
Maxwell House
74 Worship Street
London EC2A 2EN

CONTENTS

INTRODUCTION

Over the past few years there has been a quiet
revolution in the kitchen and, beginners or expert
cooks, we are all profiting by it. Cooking in fact has
never been so easy, materials have never been so
plentiful and varied as they are today. While the basic
tools like good sharp knives will always be with us,
new equipment is at our service too. The food
processor speeds the making of pâtés, soups and
sauces, mixes cakes, chops vegetables, and even
makes light pastry. The time honoured dishes remain
the same. We still make pastry for pies, soup for cold
days, meat dishes for a hungry family. But we now
have supermarkets with a bewildering display of
foodstuffs, small specialist shops for choice items, a
constant supply of fresh vegetables, new fruits we had
scarcely heard of a few years ago. There are new cuts
of meat, new fats either soft or hard as we require
them, and marvellous new foods from the freezer.

In this collection of recipes from my television
programme in *A Plus* I have tried to reflect some of the
recent changes that have so much improved the lot of
the home cook.

My thanks as always go to Clare Blunt for her calm
help in devising, preparing and testing dishes – and
especially for doing it all with a smile when so often
we are hard pressed and time is short.

Mary Berry

PASTRY
with a light touch

There is something about a perfectly baked pie, where crisp shortcrust or feathery light puff pastry, golden and shining on top, hints at the delights within. No wonder our mothers and grandmothers used to praise 'a light hand with pastry'. Nowadays you can buy yours ready made, and there is nothing wrong with that, but make it yourself and you blossom as a cook. You save money too.

Pastry divides into shortcrust and flaky or puff. Shortcrust is quick to prepare. The fat is rubbed into the flour and liquid is added – as a rough guide, use a generous tablespoonful to 4 oz (100 g) flour. Use it plain for sweet or savoury pies, tarts and flans, add sugar and egg yolk to make a rich sweet pastry. Flaky or puff pastry takes longer to make. Fat is incorporated by rolling and folding to build up layers which rise in the oven. You can speed the process by grating hard margarine into the flour. Use it for pie crust, sausage rolls, mince pies, vol au vents.

You will get better results if you let your pastry cool and set before baking.

Use fruit in season for fruit pies, or if you have a freezer, use fruit from that. I usually thaw and stew mine first. For quiches or flans I like to bake blind – that is, line the pastry case first with greaseproof paper and beans or with kitchen foil, and bake till the edges just begin to dry out. Then add the filling and the pastry will remain crisp as you finish baking it.

St Andrew's Plait (see page 10)

ST ANDREW'S PLAIT

A good family dish, serve with a gravy or basil tomato sauce. This is also very good cold and is lovely cut in thick slices to take on a picnic.

Pastry

| 8 oz (225 g) strong plain flour |
| ½ teaspoon salt |
| 6 oz (175 g) hard margarine |
| About 9 tablespoons cold water |
| A little beaten egg to glaze |

Filling

| 8 oz (225 g) minced beef |
| 8 oz (225 g) minced pork |
| 1½ oz (40 g) porridge oats |
| 1 small onion, grated |
| 1 egg |
| Salt and pepper |

For the pastry: put the flour and salt into a bowl and coarsely grate the margarine into it. Stir in just sufficient water to make a firm dough and then roll out on a lightly floured surface to make a strip about ½ inch (1.25 cm) thick and 6 inches (15 cm) wide.

Fold the pastry in three and give it a quarter turn to the left. Roll out again into a strip and fold in three. Wrap the pastry in foil and chill in the refrigerator for 30 minutes. Heat the oven to 425 deg F, 220 deg C, gas mark 7.

Place all the filling ingredients in a bowl and mix thoroughly. Roll out the pastry on a lightly floured surface into a rectangle 14 by 11 inches (35 by 27.5 cm). Place filling down the centre and make six diagonal cuts through the pastry on either side about 2 inches (5 cm) apart to within one inch (2.5 cm) of the filling.

Brush the edges of the pastry with beaten egg, then alternately cross the pastry strips over the filling to form a plait. Brush all over with a little beaten egg and then bake in the oven for about 35 minutes or until the pastry is golden brown and crisp.

Lift on to a warm serving dish.
Serves 6

BACON AND LEEK QUICHE

Use cooked lean bacon or ham for this quiche. Serve hot with French bread or with a simple salad. To get a brown underneath to the quiche put a thick metal baking sheet to heat up and bake the quiche on it.

For the flan case

| 1 oz (25 g) lard |
| 1 oz (25 g) margarine |
| 4 oz (100 g) plain flour |
| About 1 tablespoon water |

Filling

| 1 large leek |
| 1 oz (25 g) butter |
| 6 oz (175 g) lean cooked forehock of ham |
| 2 eggs |
| ¼ pint (150 ml) plain yogurt or soured cream |
| Salt and pepper |

In a bowl, rub the lard and margarine into the flour until like fine breadcrumbs. Add the water and mix until formed into a ball. Roll out on a floured surface and line an 8 inch (20 cm) flan case, fluting with your fingers all round the edge. Ideally, chill for 20 minutes. Bake blind by adding a round of greaseproof paper filled with beans, or a piece of foil first moulded round the outside of a fractionally smaller tin, for 15 to 20 minutes at 425 deg F, 220 deg, C, gas mark 7. Remove paper and beans for the last 10 minutes.

Whilst the flan case is cooking, wash and cut up the leek into small rounds and cook for a minute in a pan of melted butter, stirring all the time. Cut up the forehock into small cubes and place in a bowl. Mix with 2 eggs, the yogurt or soured cream, salt and pepper, and the cooked leeks. Put this mixture into the cooked flan case and bake in the top of the oven for 30 minutes at 350 deg F, 180 deg C, gas mark 4 until very pale golden and set.
Serves 4 to 6

KOULIBIAC

A sort of smart salmon kedgeree in a crisp puff pastry crust.

| 4 oz (100 g) long-grain rice |
| 2 oz (50 g) butter |
| 1 large onion finely chopped |
| 14 oz (397 g) can tomatoes |
| 1 lb (450 g) flaked cooked salmon |
| 2 tablespoons chopped parsley |
| Juice of 1 lemon |
| 1 teaspoon salt |
| Freshly ground black pepper |
| 14 oz (400 g) puff pastry |
| 1 beaten egg |

Serve with

| About 2 oz (50 g) butter, melted |
| Juice of half a lemon |
| ¼ pt (150 ml) soured cream |

Cook the rice in boiling salted water for about 12 minutes, then drain. Melt the butter in a pan and sauté the onion until soft. Drain the tomatoes and add to the onion and cook gently. Carefully combine the rice, onion, tomatoes, flaked salmon, parsley, cook together and moisten with the lemon juice. Add salt and pepper.

Roll out the pastry to a rectangle about 11 by 16 inches (27.5 by 40 cm). Brush with beaten egg and pile the mixture down the centre, leaving a border of pastry round the edges. Brush these with beaten egg, fold both long sides overlapping ½ inch (1.25 cm), making a fat sausage shape. Tuck the ends under the roll and decorate with pastry leaves. Place on a greased baking sheet, score across the top with a knife 3 or 4 times and brush with beaten egg. Bake in the oven at 400 deg F, 200 deg C, gas mark 6 for 30 to 45 minutes until golden. Pour melted butter and lemon juice down the scored cuts and serve with a bowl of soured cream.
Serves 6

Kidney and Mushroom Pie

RASPBERRY AND ALMOND CRUMBLE PIE

An excellent way of using up the last of the raspberries and the first wind-fall apples.

4 oz (100 g) plain flour
2 oz (50 g) ground almonds
3 oz (75 g) margarine
2 oz (50 g) light soft brown sugar
12 oz (350 g) cooking apples
12 oz (350 g) raspberries
4 oz (100 g) caster sugar
2 tablespoons water
1 oz (25 g) flaked almonds

Heat the oven to 400 deg F, 200 deg C, gas mark 6.

Put the flour in a bowl with the ground almonds, add margarine cut in small pieces and rub in with the finger tips until the mixture resembles breadcrumbs. Stir in the brown sugar.

Peel, core and slice the apples and put in a pie dish with the raspberries, caster sugar and water. Pile the crumble mixture on top of the fruit and then sprinkle with flaked almonds.

Bake in the oven for 40 minutes or until the crumble is golden brown and the apples tender. Serve with plenty of thin cream.

Serves 6

KIDNEY AND MUSHROOM PIE

Beef kidneys are always good value. Serve with a little rice and a green vegetable.

2 lb (900 g) beef kidney
1 oz (25 g) flour
1 oz (25 g) dripping
1 large onion, chopped
½ pint (300 ml) red wine
¼ pint (150 ml) stock
1 teaspoon salt
Ground black pepper
4 oz (100 g) mushrooms, sliced
8 oz (227 g) puff pastry
A little beaten egg to glaze

First cook the kidney. Remove the fat and cores and cut the kidney into small pieces. Put in a polythene bag with the flour and toss until well coated. Melt the dripping in a saucepan, add the kidney, and fry with the onion until browned. Stir in the wine, stock and seasoning and bring to the boil. Partially cover the pan and simmer for 1 hour, then stir in the mushrooms and continue cooking for another 20 minutes, or until the kidneys are tender. Check the seasoning, turn into a 1½ pint (900 ml) pie dish and allow to cool. Put a pie funnel or egg cup into the centre.

Roll out the pastry on a lightly-floured table and use to cover the pie. Seal and crimp the edges and use any pastry trimming to decorate the top with pastry leaves. Brush the pie with a little beaten egg and make a small hole in the centre. Bake in the oven at 425 deg F, 220 deg C, gas mark 7 for about 30 minutes – checking after 20 minutes and if browning too much, reduce the heat to 350 deg F, 180 deg C, gas mark 4.

Serves 6

PROFITEROLES

These are so delicious and look good.

Choux pastry

2 oz (50 g) butter

¼ pint (150 ml) water

2½ oz (62.5 g) plain flour

2 eggs, beaten

Filling

½ pint (300 ml) double cream, whipped

Icing

1½ oz (40 g) butter

1 oz (25 g) cocoa

4 oz (100 g) icing sugar, sieved

3 to 4 tablespoons evaporated milk

Heat the oven to 425 deg F, 220 deg C, gas mark 7. Grease a baking sheet. For the pastry: put the butter and water in a small saucepan, bring to the boil slowly and allow the butter to melt. Remove from the heat and add the flour all at once and beat until it forms a soft ball. Gradually beat in the eggs a little at a time to make a smooth shiny paste.

Put the mixture in a piping bag fitted with a ½ inch (1.25 cm) plain nozzle and pipe into 20 blobs on the baking sheet.

Bake in the oven for 10 minutes, then reduce the heat to 375 deg F, 190 deg C, gas mark 5 and cook for a further 15 to 20 minutes until well risen and golden brown.

Remove from the oven and split one side of each bun to allow the steam to escape. Cool on a wire rack. Fill each bun with whipped cream.

For the icing: melt the butter in a small pan and stir in the cocoa and cook gently for a minute. Remove from the heat and stir in the icing sugar and evaporated milk, beat well until starting to thicken. Dip each bun in the icing to cover the top and leave on one side to set. Then pile up in a pyramid. Serve on the same day as they are made.

Serves about 6

APPLE AND ALMOND TART

This tart is delicious served cold with pouring cream.

Pastry

6 oz (175 g) plain flour

2 oz (50 g) lard

2 oz (50 g) margarine

½ oz (12.5 g) caster sugar

2 egg yolks

Filling

4 oz (100 g) marzipan

4 oz (100 g) margarine

2 oz (50 g) caster sugar

1 lb (450 g) peeled and grated cooking apples

2 egg whites

Put the flour in a bowl, add the fats cut in small pieces and rub in until the mixture resembles fine breadcrumbs. Add the sugar and sufficient beaten egg yolk to form a firm dough. Keep the remaining yolk for the glaze. Roll out the pastry and use to line a 10 inch (25 cm) loose-bottomed flan tin. Chill. Keep any pastry trimmings, and roll out again and cut into thin strips to use for a lattice. Heat the oven to 425 deg F, 220 deg C, gas mark 7.

Knead the marzipan until soft and then roll out into a circle and cover the base of the flan.

Cream the margarine and sugar together until light and then stir in the grated apple. Whisk the egg whites until stiff and fold into the apple mixture. Spoon into the lined flan case. Arrange the pastry trimmings over the top of the flan to form a lattice and then brush with the remaining egg yolk to glaze.

Bake in the oven for about 35 to 40 minutes until a light golden brown.

Serves 8

Profiteroles

Old English Lemon Meringue Pie

OLD ENGLISH LEMON MERINGUE PIE

One of the best puddings, I think nicest served warm.

For the flan case

4 oz (100 g) plain flour

1½ oz (40 g) butter

1½ oz (40 g) lard

1 egg yolk

½ oz (12.5 g) caster sugar

Lemon filling

2 lemons

1½ oz (40 g) cornflour

½ pint (300 ml) water

2 egg yolks

3 oz (75 g) caster sugar

Meringue topping

3 egg whites

4½ oz (112 g) caster sugar

First make the pastry. Put the flour in a bowl, add the fats, cut into small pieces, and rub in with the fingertips until the mixture resembles fine breadcrumbs. Add the egg yolk and sugar and stir into the dry ingredients, binding them together. Roll out the pastry on a floured board and line an 8 inch (20 cm) flan tin. Chill for 30 minutes. Heat the oven to 425 deg F, 220 deg C, gas mark 7 with a thick baking sheet in it. Line the flan with greaseproof paper and weigh down with baking beans and bake blind for 15 to 20 minutes, taking out the paper and beans for the last 7 to 10 minutes or so, to cook the pastry through.

Meanwhile prepare the filling. Finely grate the rind and squeeze the juice from the lemons and put in a bowl with the cornflour. Boil the water and pour on to the cornflour mixture. Return it to the pan, bring to the boil and simmer for 3 minutes until thick, stirring continuously. Remove from the heat and add the egg yolks blended with sugar. Return to the heat for a moment to thicken, then cool slightly. Pour the lemon filling into the flan case.

Whisk the egg whites with an electric or rotary whisk until they form stiff peaks, add the sugar a teaspoon at a time whisking well after each addition. Spoon the meringue over the lemon filling, being careful to spread it right up to the edge of the pastry, leaving no air spaces. Return the pie to the oven and reduce the heat to 325 deg F, 160 deg C, gas mark 3 for about 30 minutes or until a pale golden brown. Serve the pie either warm or cold.

Serves 6

Making the most of
MEAT

Meat needs thinking about. These days it is the most expensive single item on the average shopping list. The important thing to remember is that the cheaper cuts of meat are of as good quality as the more expensive joints. All they need is a little time, patience, and imagination. My recipes here are not for the costly roast that is strictly for special occasions. They are designed to make the most of the cheaper cuts. Many of my favourites need long, slow cooking in a good stock – keep a supply in the freezer or use cubes – many need a variety of vegetables in a casserole or pot roast. Herbs and spices all add to the flavour, and the remains of a bottle of wine can transform a meat dish. Aim at variety. Layered beef and mozzarella cheese makes a welcome change for the family that has had too much spaghetti bolognese or lasagne. Lamb chops become festive if you bone them (two to each guest), put half a lamb's kidney between, wrap in bacon and grill quickly.

Some butchers sell casserole pork at under £1 a lb (450g). Use it for my ginger spiced pork or Smithfield barbecued pork, two good savoury meat dishes that won't break the bank. Breast of lamb or belly of pork can be roasted satisfactorily if you remove a good deal of the fat first. Ox kidney is inexpensive in a kidney and mushroom pie.

Mozarella Beef Florentine (see page 16)

MOZZARELLA BEEF FLORENTINE

Of all the meat recipes we enjoyed this the most. Do not keep hot as the spinach then loses colour and the cheese becomes tough.

2 lb (900 g) lean minced beef
14 oz (397 g) can tomatoes
2 good tablespoons tomato purée
2 cloves garlic, crushed
1 heaped teaspoon sugar
¼ pint (150 ml) beef stock
1½ teaspoons salt & freshly ground black pepper
Spinach and cheese filling
Enough water barely to cover the bottom of a large pan
Preferably 1 lb 8 oz (675 g) raw washed spinach or two 10.6 oz (about 300 g) packets of frozen cut leaf spinach
Knob of butter
2 oz (50 g) fresh white breadcrumbs
2 eggs
Salt & freshly ground black pepper
6 oz (175 g) thinly sliced Mozzarella cheese
2 oz (50 g) strong Cheddar or 1 oz (25 g) Parmesan cheese, grated
Plenty of freshly chopped parsley

Put the minced beef in a large non-stick pan and cook slowly, breaking down with a wooden spoon until the fat runs out. Then increase the heat and brown the meat. Add the remaining ingredients, and bring to the boil, then reduce the heat and simmer with the lid on for 45 minutes. Taste and check the seasoning.

Meanwhile make the filling. Pour the water into the pan, bring to the boil and cook the spinach (or as directed on the packet) until tender. Drain off excess liquid and add butter. Put the breadcrumbs, eggs and seasoning in a bowl and mix very thoroughly, then mix in the spinach. Heat the oven to 350 deg F, 180 deg C, gas mark 4. Place half the mince in the bottom of a shallow ovenproof dish about 9 by 9 inches (22.5 by 22.5 cm) and cover with the spinach followed by the thinly sliced cheese. Sprinkle on the grated cheese and pour over the remaining mince. Cover with foil, cook for 30 minutes. Remove the foil and scatter with parsley before serving with French bread.

Serves 6

BEACONSFIELD HOT POT

The traditional recipe for this has a thin gravy but I prefer this one. No need to serve any other vegetables, as it is complete on its own.

8 to 12 lean middle neck chops
2 onions, sliced
3 carrots, sliced
Salt
Freshly ground black pepper
¾ pint (450 ml) water
1 oz (25 g) margarine
1 oz (25 g) flour
1½ lb (675 g) potatoes, peeled

Heat the oven to 325 deg F, 160 deg C, gas mark 3.

Layer the middle neck chops with the onions and carrots in a 3 pint (1.7 lt) casserole, seasoning well between layers and then pour over the water. Cover the casserole and put in the oven for 1½ hours.

Remove the casserole from the oven and pour off the water. Increase the oven temperature to 350 deg F, 180 deg C, gas mark 4.

Remove any fat from the water. Melt the margarine in a saucepan, stir in the flour and cook for a minute. Take the pan from the heat and stir in the hot water until blended and smooth. Taste and check seasoning.

Arrange the sliced potatoes over the meat and vegetables and then pour over the hot sauce. Return to the oven for a further hour or until the potatoes are tender.

Serves 4 to 6

SMITHFIELD BARBECUED PORK

I can get cubed casserole pork at under £1 a lb (450 g) at my local butcher and at the supermarket in Beaconsfield too. Originally this recipe used pork chops which are excellent done in this sauce but rather more expensive.

1½ lb (675 g) casserole pork, cubed
Sauce
½ pint (300 ml) tomato ketchup
2 tablespoons brown sugar
2 tablespoons vinegar
2 tablespoons Worcestershire sauce
2 cloves garlic, crushed
1 teaspoon made mustard
Salt, ground black pepper
1 level tablespoon cornflour
¼ pint (150 ml) fresh orange juice

Put the prepared pork in a non-stick frying pan and cook slowly at first to draw out the fat, then brown quickly. Lift meat out with a slotted spoon into a casserole. Save any fat to use for frying on another occasion.

Measure sauce ingredients except orange juice and cornflour into the casserole, cover. Cook in the oven at 325 deg F, 160 deg C, gas mark 3, for 1½ hours till tender.

Mix cornflour with orange juice (the sort you buy in a carton for breakfast). Stir into casserole, reheat, stirring, to thicken. Check seasoning and serve with plenty of rice. (Allow about 3 oz (75 g) uncooked rice per person.)

Serves 4

Grilled Noisettes of Lamb

GRILLED NOISETTES OF LAMB

These make tiny chops look very special and can be prepared in advance, then just slipped under the grill. If you prefer not to use streaky bacon, leave more fat on the chop and wrap this round instead.

8 loin of lamb chops in the piece (about 1 lb 8 oz (675 g))

4 lambs' kidneys

Salt

Ground black pepper

8 thin long streaky bacon rashers

First bone the lamb. With a very sharp knife remove the skin with some of the fat from the outer side. Then carefully run the knife down close to the bone to remove ribs and backbone. Take out any gristle or extra fat, divide into eight long strips each with an eye of lean meat.

Remove skin from the kidneys, core them, cut each in half. Season both the kidneys and meat. Take each boned chop, lay it on its side and put half a kidney next to the eye of meat and wrap the long strip of rather fatty meat round the outside. Wrap a piece of bacon round the outside of each one and secure with a wooden cocktail stick.

Grill under a moderate grill for about 8 to 10 minutes, turning once until when pierced with a fine skewer the juices that flow are just clear.

Serves 4

DANISH PORK ROAST

Slow roasted pork on a mirepoix of onions and apricots with orange. Named because I first bought lean streaky pork rolled as a joint in the Danish Centre – I was so impressed with it that I created this recipe. The orange juice is the kind you buy for breakfast in litre cartons.

2 oz (50 g) dried apricot pieces
2 lb 8 oz (1.1 kg) joint thick belly pork, boned
2 medium onions, chopped
1 level tablespoon flour
¾ pint (450 ml) orange juice
2 beef stock cubes, crumbled
Salt
Ground black pepper
1 teaspoon dried sage
Freshly chopped parsley

First soak the apricots in hot water for 2 hours to soften them or do it in cold water overnight, then drain. Trim any surplus fat off the meat and put this fat in a non-stick frying pan over a low heat to draw out the fat. When there is about a tablespoon of fat in the pan, discard the fatty pieces and add the onions. Fry gently till pale golden, add flour then blend in orange juice and stock cubes. Add apricots and turn into small shallow ovenproof dish just large enough to take the pork when rolled. Sprinkle non-fatty side of the joint with seasoning and sage. Roll up and tie at one inch (2.5 cm) intervals with fine string. Stand on apricot mixture.

Slow roast at 325 deg F, 160 deg C, gas mark 3 for about 1¾ hours to 2 hours or until meat is tender. Lift off joint, keep hot. Taste the apricot mixture, adjust seasoning and if rather too thick add a little water or orange juice. Carve the pork and serve with the apricot mixture, scatter with parsley.

Serves 6

GARDENER'S POT ROAST

All you need to serve with this is plain boiled potatoes.

4 oz (100 g) haricot beans
2 lb (900 g) piece of silverside
A little plain flour
½ oz (12.5 g) dripping
2 onions, cut in wedges
2 large carrots, sliced
1 parsnip, diced
3 sticks celery, cut in short lengths
½ pint (300 ml) beef stock
¼ teaspoon mixed dried herbs
Salt and pepper

Place the beans in a bowl, cover with cold water and leave to soak overnight or for at least 8 hours. Coat the beef in flour and then melt the dripping in a saucepan and add the beef and quickly brown all over. Lift out and place on one side. Add the vegetables and drained beans to the pan and place the beef back on top. Pour over the stock and add herbs and seasoning. Bring to the boil and then cover the saucepan with a tight fitting lid.

Simmer gently for about 1½ hours or until the beef is tender. Allow 30 minutes to the 1 lb (450 g) and 30 minutes over. Lift out the meat and place on a warm serving dish.

Taste and check the seasoning in the vegetables and then either spoon around the beef or serve in a separate warm dish.

Serves 4 to 6

NORMANDY BEEF

This casserole is good too without mustard but to my mind more delicious with it. If you are a mustard addict you could add more, but taste first.

6 oz (175 g) streaky bacon or bacon pieces
1½ lb (675 g) good stewing steak, cut into cubes
1 good teaspoon salt and freshly ground black pepper to taste
1 oz (25 g) flour
½ pint (300 ml) cider
8 oz (225 g) button mushrooms, sliced
8 oz (225 g) onions, sliced
1 heaped tablespoon mustard

Heat oven to 300 deg F, 150 deg C, gas mark 2. Cut the bacon into small pieces and fry in a large non-stick pan until the fat runs. Add the cubed beef and brown on all sides. Season, sprinkle on the flour and cook, stirring continuously, for 1 minute. Add the cider, then the sliced mushrooms and onion. Bring to the boil, stirring all the time. Check the seasoning and transfer to an ovenproof casserole and cook in the oven for 2 hours until tender. Just before serving, stir in the mustard and check seasoning.

Serves 4

Ginger Spiced Pork

GINGER SPICED PORK

My butcher sells casserole pork in midweek. Alternatively, ask for shoulder pork and cut into cubes.

1 oz (25 g) flour
1½ teaspoons salt
Ground black pepper
1 level teaspoon ground ginger
1½ lb (675 g) casserole pork, cubed
1 oz (25 g) pork dripping or lard

Sauce
¼ teaspoon tabasco
14 oz (397 g) can tomatoes
4 oz (100 g) button mushrooms
1 tablespoon Worcestershire sauce
2 level tablespoons soft brown sugar
2 tablespoons vinegar
2 cloves garlic, crushed
1 bay leaf

Mix the flour, seasoning and ginger and use to coat the pork cubes. Heat dripping or lard in a large frying pan, fry the pork quickly until browned, turning frequently, and then transfer to a 2½ pint (1.4 lt) ovenproof dish. Combine all ingredients for sauce and then pour over the meat. Cover and cook at 325 deg F, 160 deg C, gas mark 3, for about 2 hours until the meat is tender. Remove the bay leaf, taste and check seasoning.

Serves 4

Secret of good
SOUP

A good stock makes a good soup. The best is made from beef bones, particularly marrow bones. Many butchers when you are buying meat will let you have the bones free. Get them sawn into pieces to fit your largest pan or casserole. I like to cook them slowly in the oven. I first brown them in the roasting tin after the meat has come out, then I put them in a large pan or casserole with water, add a bay leaf, salt and pepper, bring to the boil and simmer very gently for two to three hours or more. After that you remove the bones, strain the stock and if there are any scraps of meat left add them to the soup, or give them to the dog. Allow to cool and take off fat, which is free beef dripping. Freeze the stock or keep it in the fridge for two to three days.

Chicken stock is made in much the same way. When you have collected the carcasses of, say, three chickens in the freezer, flatten them with a rolling pin. The stock should jelly when cold.

Home made soup costs little and the keen soupmaker wastes nothing. Tops of leeks, ends of onion, clean outside leaves of brussels sprouts, these can all go into the soup towards the end of the cooking time, and the whole lot can be puréed. Or add chopped vegetables sautéed first in a little butter or dripping.

Stock cubes are invaluable and I wouldn't be without them. I use them when I have no stock and want to make soup in a hurry, or if the stock I have is a bit weak I simply add a cube.

Don't be afraid to try unusual flavours, like Stilton. And do serve cheese straws, melba toast and croûtons along with the soup.

GARDEN VEGETABLE SOUP

This soup makes the most of late summer garden vegetables. For vegetarians use a vegetable stock.

2 oz (50 g) haricot beans
1 oz (25 g) pearl barley
2 carrots
1 small turnip
1 onion
1 leek
2 oz (50 g) butter
2 cloves garlic – crushed
2 tablespoons tomato purée
4 pints (2 to 3 litres) good chicken or ham stock
1 bouquet garni (mace, parsley, thyme and bay leaf)
Salt and freshly ground pepper to taste
¼ cabbage (6 oz (175 g)) shredded
2 oz (50 g) thinly sliced green beans
Grated cheese and/or chopped parsley to garnish

Soak the pulses overnight with just enough water to cover. Next day, drain thoroughly. Prepare the vegetables. Slice the carrots and turnip into small matchsticks. Finely slice the onion and leek. Melt the butter in a large pan with a close fitting lid and gently fry the prepared vegetables for 5 minutes or until transparent.

Add the drained pulses, garlic, tomato purée, stock, bouquet garni, and seasoning. Boil rapidly for 5 minutes and then gently simmer for 1 hour with the lid on. Check the seasoning and add the cabbage and green beans and cook for a further 15 minutes. Remove the bouquet garni and serve with the chopped parsley and/or cheese.

Serves 6 to 8

FRESH WATERCRESS SOUP

A change from the usual potato and watercress.

2 bunches watercress
1½ oz (40 g) butter
8 oz (225 g) onions, finely chopped
1½ teaspoons salt
Freshly ground black pepper
1½ oz (40 g) flour
1 pint (600 ml) stock
1 pint (600 ml) milk

Wash the watercress, removing any limp pieces, and reserve a bunch of the brightest leaves to chop as garnish just before serving. Melt the butter in a large pan, add the onion, salt and pepper and cook until soft and transparent. Add the watercress and cook gently for a further few minutes. Add the flour and stir well and cook for a minute, stir in the stock, and bring to the boil to thicken. Blend in milk slowly and bring to the boil. Simmer until tender, about 10 minutes. Remove from heat and leave to cool. Purée in a blender or food processor, then reheat, and serve sprinkled with the reserved chopped watercress.

Serves 6

STILTON SOUP

A very good way of using the last of a piece of Stilton. Do not include the rind or it will be acid.

2 oz (50 g) butter
8 oz (225 g) onion, finely sliced
6 oz (175 g) Stilton, crumbled
2 oz (50 g) flour
2 pints (1.1 lt) chicken stock
1 bay leaf
Salt and black pepper
¼ pint (150 ml) single cream

Melt the butter in a saucepan and add the sliced onion. Fry gently until soft but not brown, then add the Stilton. Stir with a wooden spoon until the cheese melts to form a smooth cream.

Add the flour and cook for a further 5 minutes, stirring continuously. Add the stock, bay leaf and seasoning and bring to the boil, stirring. Simmer for 20 minutes. Remove the bay leaf, taste and check seasoning, then add the cream and serve at once.

Serves 6

Top: *Garden Vegetable Soup*

Centre: *Italian Carrot Soup*

Bottom: *Stilton Soup*

French Onion Soup

FRENCH ONION SOUP

Adding a little sugar when frying onions helps them to caramelise and turn a lovely pale golden colour.

1½ lb (675 g) onions
3 oz (75 g) butter
2 teaspoons sugar
1½ oz (40 g) plain flour
3 pints (1.7 lt) chicken or beef stock
1 level teaspoon salt
Ground black pepper
6 slices French bread, ½ inch (1.25 cm) thick
4 oz (100 g) Gruyère cheese

Peel and thinly slice the onions. Melt half the butter in a large saucepan and add the onions and sugar. Cook over low heat for about 15 minutes, until the onions are soft and pale golden brown. Stir in the flour and cook, stirring for a few minutes. Add the stock and salt and pepper and bring to the boil. Place the lid on and simmer the soup for about 30 minutes, until onion is tender.

Meanwhile butter both sides of each slice of French bread with the remaining butter. Grate the cheese and sprinkle half over the bread.

Bake the bread on a baking tray, in a pre-heated oven, at 350 deg F, 180 deg C, gas mark 4, until the bread is crisp and the cheese has melted, or do this under the grill turning once before putting the cheese on and browning.

Arrange the bread in individual bowls and pour over the hot onion soup. Serve remaining grated cheese in a separate bowl.

Serves 6

SHERRIED KIDNEY SOUP

A sturdy soup, good before something like cauliflower cheese.

1 lb (450 g) young ox kidney
2 large onions
1 oz (25 g) butter
2 level tablespoons flour
¼ teaspoon mixed herbs
3 pints (1.7 lt) good beef stock
Salt
Ground black pepper
1 tablespoon redcurrant jelly
6 tablespoons sherry
Chopped parsley

Take off any skin from the kidney, then remove cores and slice into rough cubes. Slice onions. Melt butter, fry kidney and onion together until onion is soft. Stir in flour and herbs, blend well. Add stock, seasoning and redcurrant jelly. Bring to the boil, cover and simmer very gently for about 1½ hours until kidney is tender. Purée the soup in a blender or processor. Reheat, add sherry, taste and adjust seasoning. Serve with a sprinkling of parsley.

Serves 6

ITALIAN CARROT SOUP

A glorious brightly coloured soup.

2 lb (900 g) carrots
1 large red pepper
2 cloves garlic, crushed
Zest and juice of half a lemon
2 pints (1.1 lt) chicken stock
Salt and black pepper
½ pint (300 ml) cream

Scrub and roughly cut up the carrots. De-seed the pepper and chop. Put in a large saucepan with the garlic, lemon, stock, salt and pepper and bring to the boil. Simmer for ½ an hour till tender. Cool, purée in a processor or blender until smooth. Rinse out the saucepan and pour the soup through a sieve into it. Add the cream and bring back just to the boil. Check seasoning. Serve at once.

Serves 6

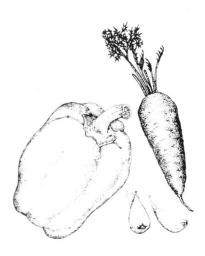

Good things to go with Soup

CHEESEY FRENCH BREAD

Cream 1 oz (25 g) butter with a crushed clove of garlic and 2 oz (50 g) grated cheese until well mixed and then spread over 4 thick slices of French stick loaf. Grill until golden brown and serve on individual soup portions.

CHEESE STRAWS OR TWISTS

4 oz (100 g) plain flour

2 oz (50 g) butter

Salt and cayenne pepper

2 oz (50 g) Cheddar cheese, grated

1 egg yolk

1 tablespoon cold water

Heat the oven to 400 deg F, 200 deg C, gas mark 6.

Put the flour in a bowl and rub in the butter, until it forms fine crumbs, season well and stir in cheese. Blend the egg yolk with the water and add to the pastry to form a dough. Roll out to ¼ inch (0.60 cm) thick and cut into straws about 2½ inches (6.25 cm) long and ¼ inch (0.60 cm) wide.

Place on a greased baking sheet, twisting if liked, and bake in the oven for about 10 to 15 minutes until a light golden brown. Serve with soup.

CROÛTONS

Take day old white, preferably ready sliced, bread. Cut into pencil sized strips, cut again to form cubes. Don't bother to take the crusts off the slices first. Deep fry until golden brown, lift out with a slotted spoon and drain on kitchen paper. Allow half a slice of bread per portion of croûtons.

Croûtons freeze well. If a large amount is prepared at one time, store in the freezer and take out when required and warm in the oven.

HERBY PIN WHEELS

Combine 4 oz (100 g) butter with 2 tablespoons fresh chopped herbs. Spread over slices of thin sliced white bread with the crusts removed. Any butter not used can be stored in the refrigerator until another day. Roll up the slices of bread into a thin sausage and cut into slices. Grill or bake until crispy. Allow 3 minutes under the grill and about 10 minutes in the oven.

MELBA TOAST

Traditionally made by toasting thin slices of bread on both sides. Then carefully with a very sharp knife split the slices through the centre and toast the uncooked sides until crisp and slightly curled.

FRUITS
of the world

Avocados, once a rare treat, have become something
of a commonplace, if that is the word to use for
anything so good. Today mangoes and guavas,
lychees and pawpaws are appearing in supermarkets
and small greengrocers' shops alike and we have a lot
of pleasure in trying them out. It is the development of
new growing methods, swift chilled transport and up
to date packing methods that have made possible this
revolution in our eating habits, and there has never
been such a variety of fruit on sale in this country as
there is now.

Take citrus fruits. There were once lemons and
grapefruit, oranges and tangerines. Now there is an
enormous variety of orange and tangerine crosses,
there are ugli fruits, and pink grapefruit. There are all
kinds of melon, there are fresh dates and figs. A fruit
salad today presents a bewildering choice. I like a
mixture of the familiar and the unusual in mine, and I
use canned fruit as well. The fruit should not be
chopped too small and I think it looks best arranged
in layers preferably in a deep glass dish. I do not
as a rule skin and de-pip the grapes, but if you have
time to do this, a new hairgrip is a useful tool for
getting the pips out.

My recipe for frugal marmalade uses all those bits of
peel that are usually thrown away. I store orange,
lemon and grapefruit skins in the freezer and boil them
up with a can of concentrated Spanish citrus fruit pulp.
It makes a very economical marmalade.

LAYERED FRUIT SALAD

Layering the fruits in a straight sided glass dish, looks exciting and tastes beautifully fresh. Keep the fruits in large pieces and contrasting colours.

Syrup

4 oz (100 g) caster sugar
¼ pint (150 ml) water
Juice of half a lemon

2 pears
8 oz (225 g) strawberries
6 oz (175 g) black grapes
6 oz (175 g) green grapes
1 mango
1 small pineapple
1 kiwi fruit

First make the syrup. Put the sugar and water in a saucepan and bring to the boil, stirring until the sugar has dissolved. Boil for a minute then remove from the heat and add the lemon juice. Cool.

Peel, core and slice the pears and put in the base of a glass dish. Reserve three strawberries for the top of the salad and then hull the remainder and put on top of the pears.

Cut the grapes in half and remove the pips. Add to the bowl, keeping the black grapes and green grapes in separate layers.

Score the skin of the mango downwards from the non-stick end into one inch (2.5 cm) sections and then pull the skin down in strips like peeling a banana. Slice the fruit, cutting right through to the stone, then across in pieces and lay on top of the grapes.

Peel, core and chop the pineapple and add to the dish.

Finally, peel the kiwi fruit and cut into thin slices and arrange round the edge of the dish and put the three whole strawberries in the centre.

Pour over the sugar syrup, cover the dish with cling film and chill in the refrigerator for several hours. Serve with a bowl of thick cream.

Serves 8

MANGO ICE CREAM

A lovely pale golden, unusual ice cream. It can be served with fresh mango slices.

1 ripe mango
4 eggs, separated
4 oz (100 g) caster sugar
½ pint (300ml) double cream

Peel the mango and remove the stone and rub through a sieve. Whisk the egg yolks in a bowl until blended.

In a larger bowl, whisk the egg whites until stiff, then whisk in the sugar a teaspoon at a time. Whisk the cream in a small bowl until it forms soft peaks and fold into the egg white mixture with the mango purée until well mixed. Turn into a 2½ pint (1.4lt) container.

Cover, label, and freeze until solid.

Leave to thaw at room temperature for 10 minutes before serving scoopfuls in small glass dishes with crisp thin biscuits.

Serves 8

Mango Ice Cream

Opposite page: *Layered Fruit Salad*

PASSION CUPS

A rather special dessert, a very good way of using up those awkward broken meringue shells.

4 passion fruit

½ pint (300 ml) double cream

3 meringue shells (see page 55), roughly broken up

Halve the passion fruit and scoop out the flesh and then sieve to remove the seeds. Whisk the cream until it forms soft peaks and then stir in the passion fruit and lastly fold in the broken meringue shells.

Divide the mixture among 4 glasses or small cups and chill until required.

Serves 4

FRUGAL MARMALADE

Have you ever thought it is a shame to throw away those citrus fruit skins? Well don't. Keep all the fruit skins in one bag in the freezer – add to them after you have had a grapefruit for breakfast, used the juice of an orange or lemon for a cake. Keep satsuma skins too. First take out any surplus white pithy skin before adding to the bag in the freezer, there isn't much in a satsuma but there is lots in a grapefruit. Then use them for this marmalade made from canned lemon pulp. I used the marmalade prepared lemons or you could use a can of prepared Seville oranges. If you like a dark marmalade use ¼ muscovado – dark brown sugar. For ginger marmalade add 8 oz (225 g) chopped preserved stem ginger just before potting.

The basic recipe

1 lb (450 g) mixed citrus fruit peels (grapefruit, orange, ugli, limes, lemon, satsuma or what have you)

1¾ pints (1 lt) water

6 lb (2.7 kg) sugar

1 lb 13 oz can (823 g) Mamade prepared lemons

Take frozen peels from the freezer, thaw enough to slice the larger peels such as the grapefruit into 4 and the rest in halves. Put in a large preserving pan, add 1 pint (600 ml) of the water, cover tightly with a lid or a piece of foil. Bring to the boil and simmer very gently until peels are tender. Keep an eye on them so they don't boil dry; the liquid needs to reduce to ½ pint (300 ml). Lift out peel with a slotted spoon and chop up with a sharp knife just as thick as you like. The liquid in the pan should be ½ pint (300 ml), if not, reduce accordingly.

Return peel to the pan, add lemon pulp, the remaining ¾ pint (450 ml) of water and the sugar, and slowly bring to the boil, stirring, without the lid. Then boil rapidly for 20 minutes, test for setting by putting a small teaspoon of the marmalade on a cold saucer. Leave to cool. If it wrinkles when pushed with the finger it is set, if not, return pan to heat and boil a few minutes more.

Pour into jars after about 10 minutes cooling. Cover and label.

Makes about 10 lb (4.5 kg)

N.B. You can soften the peels in a pressure cooker or slow oven but you should always end up with ½ pint (300 ml) liquid.

Key Lime Pie

KEY LIME PIE

A speciality of the Key West, Florida, where the key limes are grown. You will find it in every restaurant and bar in Florida.

Biscuit crumb case

5 oz (150 g) digestive biscuits

2½ oz (62.5 g) butter

1 oz (25 g) demerara sugar

Filling

2 eggs, separated

7 oz (200 g) can condensed milk

Grated rind and juice of 2 limes

Preheat the oven to 350 deg F, 180 deg C, gas mark 4.

Place the biscuits in a plastic bag and roll with a rolling pin to make fine crumbs. Melt the butter in a saucepan, then add the biscuits and sugar. Stir well together, then place in a 9 inch (22.5 cm) loose-bottomed flan tin, pressing over the base and up the sides to form a shell.

Beat together the egg yolks and condensed milk. Add the grated rind and juice from the limes and stir until thick. Whisk the egg whites until stiff and fold into the lime mixture. Pour into the biscuit shell and bake for 20 to 30 minutes until set and just beginning to colour at the edges.

If you prefer, this can be made in a pastry pie shell that has previously been baked blind.

Serves 6

CURRIED FRESH FRUIT SLAW

A salad that goes particularly well with ham and beef.

3 tablespoons mayonnaise

3 tablespoons French dressing

¼ teaspoon Dijon mustard

¼ teaspoon curry powder

2 teaspoons mango chutney juice

2 pears, peeled, cored and chopped

6 oz (175 g) mixed black and green grapes, seeded

Half a fresh pineapple, peeled, cored and chopped

8 oz (225 g) white cabbage, finely shredded

Place the mayonnaise, French dressing, mustard, curry powder and mango chutney juice in a large bowl and stir until blended. Add the fruit and cabbage and toss in the dressing until evenly coated. Turn into a serving dish, cover with cling film and chill for about one hour before serving to allow the flavours to blend.

Serves 6 with other salads

Cooking with
CREAM

Is cream an extravagance? I don't think it is, not if you use it wisely. Cream enriches any dish, whether it is meat, fish, chicken, vegetables. It adds something special to any sauce, sweet or savoury, and a spoonful in scrambled eggs just as you take the pan off the heat makes everybody's favourite supper dish into a treat.

When I am planning a menu I take care to have cream in one course only. If I am using it in the goulash for the main course I serve a light fruity pudding afterwards; if I am adding it to the soup then I do not make a creamy sauce for the fish. And I do not use it every day.

Cream used to be either single or double. Now there is a bewildering variety on the market and a confusion of different names – whipping cream, spooning cream, half cream – and even cream in an aerosol for decorating cakes and puddings. There is also soured cream which has a sharp, fresh taste and is very useful in cooking. Don't be afraid that this is cream that has gone bad, it has been specially prepared. You can do it yourself by adding lemon juice to fresh single cream. Use it in boeuf stroganoff and other meat dishes. And if you make your own cream from unsalted butter you will save at least half the cost.

Single cream is probably the most satisfactory to use for general purposes, where whipping is not required. When you are putting it in savoury sauces, do not let the sauce reboil or the cream may separate and curdle.

Turkey Stroganoff (see page 34)

TURKEY STROGANOFF

Quick and special. Prepare ingredients, cook at the last moment and serve at once.

About 1 lb (450 g) turkey breast or chicken breast
1 tablespoon corn oil
1 oz (25 g) butter
1 medium onion, sliced
4 oz (100 g) mushrooms, sliced
1 tablespoon tomato purée
½ pint (300 ml) soured cream
Salt and freshly ground black pepper

Cut the turkey or chicken breasts into long thin strips. Measure oil and butter into a large frying pan and fry the onion until lightly browned. Add the turkey or chicken, fry until browned on all sides, then add mushrooms, toss with meat and stir for a minute. Mix tomato purée with soured cream, add to pan and stir. Season with salt and pepper. Heat until piping hot – do not boil. Serve at once with rice or noodles and a green vegetable.

Serves 4

GOULASH

A true Hungarian goulash has potato added too but I prefer it without. Serve with rice or potatoes.

1½ lb (675 g) chuck steak
2 oz (50 g) bacon fat or dripping
1 lb (450 g) onions, sliced
1 pint (600 ml) beef stock
1 teaspoon salt
3 heaped tablespoons tomato purée
2 level teaspoons caster sugar
1½ oz (40 g) flour
4 level tablespoons paprika
5 oz (150 ml) carton soured cream

Remove any fat and gristle from meat, then cut the meat into medium-sized cubes. Melt the bacon fat or dripping in a heavy based oven-proof dish, add the onions and meat and cook over a moderate heat until the meat is sealed and the onions golden brown. Pour over the stock, season with salt and bring to the boil.

Meanwhile blend the tomato purée, sugar, flour and paprika in a small bowl with a few tablespoons of the hot stew liquid. Bring back to the boil, cover and cook in a moderate oven 325 deg F, 160 deg C, gas mark 3 for about 2 hours until tender. Just before serving check seasoning and stir in the soured cream.

Serves 4 to 6

CHICKEN WITH SWISS LEMON SAUCE

A divine sauce that really needs to be served with creamed potatoes or rice and bright green vegetables such as broccoli or courgettes.

6 chicken breasts (boneless without skin)
Salt and freshly ground black pepper
1 tablespoon corn or vegetable oil
2 oz (50 g) butter
2 level tablespoons plain flour
15 oz (425 g) can consommé
2 eggs
Juice of 1 lemon
Chopped parsley

Take a very sharp knife and split each breast in half, making two flat fillets. Season with salt and pepper. Heat the oil and butter together in a non-stick pan and cook the chicken until golden brown on both sides. Lift out on to a plate and keep hot, add the flour to the remaining fat, stir well. Add the consommé, stir well and bring to the boil, cover and simmer for 5 minutes over a low heat. Cool slightly.

Beat the eggs and lemon juice together in a bowl and stir in the consommé. Return everything to the pan, heat slowly over a low heat (stirring continuously), until thickened. Do not boil otherwise it will separate. Check seasoning. Pour over chicken breasts, serve immediately, or keep warm in a very low oven. Sprinkle with chopped parsley.

Serves 6

ESCALOPES OF VEAL WITH MUSHROOMS AND WHITE WINE

Very special yet very easy to make.

4 escalopes of veal or 4 chicken breasts
1 oz (25 g) butter
8 oz (225 g) button mushrooms, sliced
¼ pint (150 ml) white wine
½ pint (300 ml) double cream
Salt
Freshly ground black pepper
Chopped parsley

Put the veal escalopes or chicken breasts between 2 sheets of cling film and beat them fairly flat with a rolling pin. Melt the butter in a large frying pan and fry the escalopes on each side for 2 to 3 minutes until golden brown. Add the sliced mushrooms and continue to sauté until they are cooked.

Remove the meat and mushrooms from the pan, place on a serving dish and keep warm. Add the white wine to the pan and stir into the juices and cook until it reduces in quantity by half. Add the double cream and cook for a few minutes, until it reduces to a thick creamy sauce. Season with salt and pepper and pour the sauce over the veal or chicken. Sprinkle with parsley and serve with rice or noodles and a green vegetable.

Serves 4

Creamy Fish Pie

HEAVENLY POTATOES

Choose a waxy potato – Desiree I find is ideal.

2 lb (900 g) even-sized potatoes
Salt
Ground black pepper
1½ oz (40 g) butter, melted
¼ pint (150 ml) single cream

Boil the potatoes in their skins until barely tender and still firm in the centre, drain and leave to get really cold. Ideally boil the day before required. Butter a 2 pint (1 lt) shallow ovenproof dish really well.

Peel the skins off the potatoes and lightly grate the potato into the dish on the coarse grater. Season well between the layers and do not press down. Pour over the melted butter and cream.

Cook in the oven at 425 deg F, 220 deg C, gas mark 7 for 20 to 25 minutes until crisp and golden brown.

Serves 6

HOME MADE CREAM

Cream is very expensive, so I often make this one in the blender and nobody seems to notice that it is not fresh cream.

8 oz (225 g) unsalted butter
½ pint (300 ml) milk
Scant level teaspoon powdered gelatine

Cut the butter into small pieces. Put the milk in a saucepan and sprinkle on the gelatine and leave for three minutes.

Add the butter to the saucepan and heat until the butter has just melted. Pour into a blender or processor and switch on to maximum speed for 30 seconds until blended. Pour into a jug and chill before serving cold after stirring.

Makes just under one pint (600 ml) cream.

CREAMY FISH PIE

This reheats beautifully but it is best not to freeze for longer than a week as it contains chopped hard boiled eggs.

2 lb (900 g) cod fillets
About ½ pint (300 ml) cider
Milk
1½ oz (40 g) butter
1½ oz (40 g) flour
¼ pint (150 ml) single cream
2 teaspoons salt
Freshly ground black pepper
3 hard boiled eggs, chopped
2 tablespoons chopped parsley
2 lb (900 g) potatoes – mashed with milk and a little butter

Put the cod fillets in a large pan, add cider and simmer for about 5 minutes until just cooked – the flesh should be white. Lift the fish from the pan, remove the skin and any bones and flake into a 3 pint (1.7 lt) shallow ovenproof dish. Pour the cider back into a measuring jug and make up to ¾ pint (450 ml) with milk.

Melt the butter in the pan, add the flour and cook and then bring to the boil with cider and milk. Stir until it thickens, Add the cream, salt and pepper, eggs and chopped parsley and simmer gently until well mixed. Pour over the flaked fish and mix well. Cool. Top with soft, seasoned mashed potatoes and cook in the oven, 375 deg F, 190 deg C, gas mark 5 for about 40 minutes until golden brown.

Serves 6

CRÈME BRÛLÉE

Very rich, but amazingly easy to make. Good to serve with fresh fruit salad.

4 egg yolks

1 oz (25 g) caster sugar or vanilla sugar

1 pint (600 ml) single cream

2 oz (50 g) demerara sugar

Heat the oven to 325 deg F, 160 deg C, gas mark 3. Butter well a shallow 1½ pint (900 ml) oven proof dish. Beat the egg yolks with the sugar or vanilla sugar – if you have no vanilla sugar, add a little vanilla essence. Heat the cream to scalding (just too hot to put your finger in) and gradually beat on to the egg yolks and sugar. Pour through a sieve into the dish. Stand it in a baking tin half filled with warm water and bake in the oven for 45 minutes or until set.

Take out and leave to cool, then place in the refrigerator for several hours. Sprinkle the top with the demerara sugar and put under a hot grill. Watch carefully until the sugar melts and then caramelises to a golden brown. Remove and chill for about 3 hours before serving.
Serves 4 to 6

Crème Brûlée

BRANDY SYLLABUB

Very easy, but very rich. Serve it in small dishes, glasses or old fashioned small coffee cups. Goes very well with brandy snaps.

½ pint (300 ml) double cream

1 to 2 tablespoons lemon juice

3 tablespoons brandy

1 to 2 oz (25 to 50 g) caster sugar

Place all the ingredients in a bowl and whisk together until light and the mixture will hold a soft peak. Turn into four small dishes or glasses and chill thoroughly.
Serves 4

Athol Brose

MILLE FEUILLES

These are delicious but messy to eat and are best tackled with a fork.

14 oz (397 g) packet puff pastry

½ pint (300 ml) whipping cream, whipped

Raspberry jam

4 oz (100 g) icing sugar, sieved

A little lemon juice

Heat the oven to 450 deg F, 230 deg C, gas mark 8.

Roll pastry to a square 12 by 12 inches (30 by 30cm) and cut into three long strips 12 by 4 inches (30 by 10cm). Place each on a baking tray and prick well. Bake in the oven for about 15 minutes until well risen and golden brown. Cool on a wire rack.

Lay the three pieces of pastry on top of each other and trim so that they are an even size. Lay flat and then place one on a large serving dish and spread with jam, then cover with half the cream. Lay a second piece of pastry on top and spread that with jam and the remaining cream. Put the last piece of pastry on top and press down lightly but firmly.

Put the icing sugar in a bowl and stir in just sufficient lemon juice to form a soft icing and then spread over the top of the mille feuilles and leave to set. Serve either whole or if preferred cut into 8 portions before serving.
Serves 8

ATHOL BROSE

The Scots of course love whisky, and this is a favourite. Serve in individual glasses or ramekins. It can be made with all double cream, but my version is less rich and not quite so thick.

½ pint (300 ml) double cream

½ pint (300 ml) plain yogurt

4 tablespoons thin honey

About 4 tablespoons whisky

Whisk the cream until thick and then blend in the yogurt and honey. Add the whisky and then taste and, if liked, you could add a very little more.

Turn into six glasses, use champagne glasses if you have them. Serve at once.
Serves 6

CHOCOLATE
–they love it

Chocolate is top favourite with young and old alike and practically guarantees the success of a dish. It is versatile, which means that there are plenty of opportunities for enjoying it. It goes into puddings hot and cold, cakes, mousses, ice cream, meringues, sweets of all kinds. It can make a simple sauce for the children to pour over ice cream, or a sophisticated soufflé flavoured with brandy or rum for the grown-ups. And a good chocolate cake recipe is in constant demand.

The best for most cooking purposes is plain. I like to use something like Bourneville, a real plain chocolate with a good flavour, dark and strong. If you use cocoa for an even stronger taste, it is best mixed with a little hot water before adding to the other ingredients to bring out the full flavour. Drinking chocolate contains added sugar and is much milder in taste. Cooking chocolate sold in blocks is cheaper, because it is not real chocolate. Use it for less expensive recipes or for making decorations like chocolate curls to put on puddings or cakes.

It is easy to melt chocolate – only too easy if you happen to leave some on a sunny windowsill on a hot day. A more satisfactory, and less messy, way is to put pieces of chocolate in a small bowl over a pan of hot water and let it melt *slowly*. Small amounts can be melted in a strong polythene bag in a warm place. Then, when the right consistency is reached, just snip a corner of the bag and the chocolate is ready for pouring.

Colettes and Chocolate Brandy Truffles (see page 40)

CHOCOLATE BRANDY TRUFFLES

These make good presents. Keep in the refrigerator – right at the back so they are not too tempting!

6 oz (175 g) plain chocolate

3 oz (75 g) butter

3 level tablespoons golden syrup

4 tablespoons brandy

4 oz (100 g) ground almonds

12 oz (350 g) madeira cake, crumbled

Chocolate vermicelli or crushed chocolate flakes

About 50 small paper sweet cases

Break the chocolate into pieces and place with the butter and golden syrup in a bowl over a pan of hot water. Heat gently to melt the chocolate. Remove bowl from the heat and stir in the brandy, ground almonds and cake crumbs and mix well. Chill, to firm the mixture, so it is easier to handle.

Spread the vermicelli or crushed chocolate flakes into a shallow dish. Take a rounded teaspoon of the mixture, shaped into a ball, and roll and coat evenly in the vermicelli or flakes. Place each in a paper case and leave in a cool place to become really firm.

Makes about 50

COLETTES

Tricky to make but worth the effort. First you line tiny wax sweet paper-cases with chocolate, then add a rich chocolate mocha filling.

The chocolate cases

3½ oz (100 g) bar plain chocolate, broken into small pieces

The filling

5 oz (150 g) plain chocolate broken into small pieces

5 tablespoons water

1 level teaspoon instant coffee powder

2 oz (50 g) butter, softened

2 egg yolks

About 1 teaspoon rum

You will need 10 to 12 waxed paper sweet cases.

First make the chocolate cases. Put the chocolate into a bowl placed over a pan of hot water and leave it to melt. When it has melted, remove the bowl from the heat and use to line the insides of the paper cases.

Spread the chocolate round the base and sides of each case, using the handle of a teaspoon to make a smooth coating. Put the cases in the refrigerator to set. Meanwhile prepare the filling. Put the chocolate, water and coffee powder into a bowl standing over a pan of hot water. Stir until melted and then allow to cool. Beat in the butter a little at a time, then blend in the egg yolks and rum. Leave in a cold place until it has thickened and is completely cold.

When the chocolate cases have set, peel off the cases very carefully, one at a time, leaving the remaining cases in the refrigerator and returning the chocolate to the refrigerator. (The chocolate melts very quickly unless kept cold.) Put the filling into a piping bag fitted with a large rose nozzle and pipe the filling into each of the chocolate cases to fill them. Store them in the refrigerator and if you are giving them as presents, suggest that they are kept in the refrigerator.

Makes 10 to 12

FAMILY CHOCOLATE CAKE

For many years I have been making a chocolate cake with oil in it. It started off as Express Chocolate Cake. This one is a first cousin, but keeps better and has a more pronounced chocolate flavour too. The icing and filling is a thin layer but fairly rich.

6½ oz (187.5 g) self-raising flour

1 teaspoon baking powder

5 oz (150 g) caster sugar

2 eggs

5 oz (150 g) hard margarine melted and cooled

¼ pint (150 ml) milk

2 tablespoons golden syrup

2 rounded tablespoons cocoa, sieved

Icing and filling

3 oz (75 g) margarine

2 rounded tablespoons cocoa, sieved

1 rounded tablespoon golden syrup

About 2 tablespoons apricot jam

Chocolate flake or curls

Heat the oven to 325 deg F, 160 deg C, gas mark 3. Grease and line two 8 inch (20 cm) sandwich tins with greased greaseproof paper. Beat all the ingredients together until smooth. Divide between the tins and bake in the oven for 40 minutes or until cake springs back when pressed and comes away from the sides. Remove from oven, turn out on to a wire rack. Cool and then remove the paper. Spread one half with apricot jam.

For the icing and filling, cream all ingredients together in a saucepan over a low heat. Cool. When just beginning to thicken, spread half in the middle of the 2 sponges on top of the jam, and the rest on top of the cake. Decorate with flake chocolate or chocolate curls if liked.

Chocolate Marron Blessing

CHOCOLATE MARRON BLESSING

Very rich, so serve very thin slices with cream. It freezes well, thaw several hours in the refrigerator before serving.

To line a 2 lb (900 g) loaf tin

2 tablespoons brandy

2 tablespoons water

About 28 sponge fingers

Marron filling

3½ oz (100 g) bar plain chocolate

4 oz (100 g) unsalted butter, softened

6 oz (175 g) caster sugar

15½ oz (439 g) unsweetened chestnut purée

For decoration

¼ pint (150 ml) whipped cream

Few golden almonds or chocolate flake

Measure the brandy and water into a flattish soup plate. Dip each biscuit quickly in this – the unsugared side only. The sugared side should remain dry and crisp. Take a 2 lb (900 g) loaf tin and line the base with the sponge fingers dipped in brandy and water, sugar side towards the tin. Cut the remainder of the biscuits in half and follow the same process, and stand them up all the way round the tin.

Now make the marron filling. Break the chocolate into pieces and put in a bowl standing over hot water and allow to melt slowly. Cream butter and sugar together until light. Mash the chestnut purée down in a separate bowl till smooth, add to the creamed butter and sugar. Cool chocolate slightly and add to the creamed mixture. Turn into the centre of the sponge fingers, level the top and chill until firm, or freeze.

This needs to be turned out and be served very cold. Decorate with whipped cream and golden almonds or chocolate flake.

Serves 8 to 10

Irresistible Chocolate Cake

IRRESISTIBLE CHOCOLATE CAKE

A divine feather-light chocolate cake, dark, spongy and moist, made without fat or flour. Best eaten with a fork either for tea or dessert. Keep in the refrigerator for up to 3 days. It also freezes well for up to 3 weeks.

Cake

6 large eggs

5 oz (150 g) caster sugar, warmed

2 oz (50 g) cocoa, sieved

Filling and topping

1½ oz (40 g) cooking chocolate

½ pint (300 ml) whipping cream, whipped

Heat oven to 350 deg F, 180 deg C, gas mark 4. Grease and line with greased greaseproof paper two 8 inch (20 cm) sandwich tins.

First separate the eggs, putting the whites in a large bowl and the yolks in a smaller bowl. Add caster sugar and cocoa to the yolks, whisk until thick. Whisk whites with a hand rotary or electric whisk until the mixture forms stiff peaks. Add 2 tablespoons of the whisked whites to the yolks. Mix together then add this yolk mixture to the egg whites and fold with a metal spoon until the mixture is one even colour.

Gently turn into the tins and bake in the oven for about 25 minutes until just beginning to shrink back from the sides of the tins. Leave to cool in the tins for 5 minutes. The cake will sink a little on cooling, so expect it!

Turn on to wire racks and remove paper. While they are cooling, make chocolate curls.

Melt chocolate in pan over hot water. Spread out on a marble or laminated table top. Spread thinly with a palate knife. Leave to just set. Then with a French cook's knife at an angle of 45 degrees push the knife forward to make chocolate curls.

Sandwich cakes together with half the cream, spread the rest on the top. Lift chocolate curls on to the top. Keep cake cool until served.

Serves 8 to 10

CHOCOLATE AND HAZELNUT TORTE

When placing the sponge fingers around the edge of the tin, stand them at a slight slant, then when you get to the last one gently push them all upright. As soon as you start pouring in the chocolate mixture it will be easier to make sure they all stand upright around the edge of the tin.

2 oz (50 g) shelled hazelnuts
2 oz (50 g) caster sugar
3 eggs
3½ oz (100 g) bar plain chocolate
½ oz (12.5 g) powdered gelatine
4 tablespoons cold water
½ pint (300 ml) double cream
3 tablespoons orange juice
3 tablespoons rum
28 sponge fingers
Decoration
¼ pint (150 ml) double cream

Reserve 12 whole hazelnuts for decoration, chop the remainder. Warm the sugar on an ovenproof plate or a piece of foil, then pour into a bowl with the eggs and whisk on the highest speed with an electric or rotary whisk until stiff enough to leave a trail.

Break the chocolate into pieces and place in a bowl over a pan of hot water until melted. Place the gelatine and water in a small bowl or cup and leave to stand for a few minutes to form a sponge, then stand in a pan of simmering water until dissolved, remove from the heat and leave to cool. Whisk the cream until it holds a soft peak, add the chopped nuts, cooled chocolate and gelatine. Fold this chocolate mixture into the eggs and sugar.

Mix together the orange juice and rum in a flattish dish. Dip the unsugared sides of the sponge fingers into this and arrange sugared side out in an 8 inch (20 cm) round deep cake tin until there is a complete circle

around the sides. Pour in the chocolate mixture and level off the sponge fingers to the top of the chocolate mixture, and arrange the trimmings all over the top.

Cover the top of the tin with foil and chill until firm.

To serve, dip the tin quickly in hot water and then turn out the torte on to a serving dish. Decorate the top with the ¼ pint (150 ml) double cream whipped until thick and place the 12 reserved hazelnuts evenly around the edge.

Serves 8

DARK FROZEN CHOCOLATE MOUSSE

A beautifully written card was thrust into my hand with this very easy chocolate mousse. I have made the method foolproof by making the meringue my way.

3½ oz (100 g) bar plain chocolate
1 level tablespoon cocoa
1 level teaspoon instant coffee powder
2 tablespoons water
8 egg whites
3 oz (75 g) caster sugar

Break up chocolate and put in a bowl over a pan of gently simmering water. Mix together the cocoa, instant coffee and water, add to the melted chocolate and beat together thoroughly until creamy. Whisk the egg whites until stiff and add sugar a teaspoon at a time, whisking all the time on maximum speed. Fold in the chocolate mixture until all is absorbed and the mixture smooth.

Pour into strengthened straight-sided glass bowl (2 pint, 1.1 lt) or fill 6 to 8 ramekin dishes. Store in the freezer for up to 10 days. After this time the mousse begins to shrink down a little from the dish.

Serve still frozen and with a little single cream.

Serves 6 to 8

MILK CHOCOLATE CRUNCHIES

Children like making these and eveyone, including their fathers, loves them.

6 oz (175 g) milk chocolate
5 oz (150 g) hard margarine
1 egg
1 oz (25 g) caster sugar
6 oz (175 g) digestive biscuits
1 oz (25 g) chopped almonds
2 oz (50 g) sultanas
1 oz (25 g) glacé cherries, quartered
15 paper cake cases

Break the chocolate into pieces and melt with the margarine in a bowl over a pan of simmering water. Beat egg and sugar together well, and gradually add the melted chocolate mixture. Break up the biscuits until quite small, but not crumbled, and stir in along with the almonds, sultanas and cherries. Pour into the paper cake cases. Chill overnight.

Makes about 15

RICH CHOCOLATE SAUCE

Serve with vanilla ice cream or poured over bananas.

4 oz (100 g) caster sugar
3 tablespoons golden syrup
2 oz (50 g) plain chocolate, broken in small pieces
6 oz (170 g) can evaporated milk

Place all the ingredients in a non-stick saucepan and very slowly heat until the mixture comes to the boil, then simmer until all the ingredients have melted and blended together. Cool, stirring occasionally. Store in a container in the refrigerator and use within four weeks

Makes about ½ pint (300 ml) sauce.

CHICKEN
–everybody's meat

Chickens are on most tables today. Modern methods of rearing and refrigeration have made birds of uniform quality available all over the country and we eat more of them probably than any other meat. Most people now buy frozen ones which are inexpensive and ready to cook. You can buy whole birds or chicken pieces. For a family a whole bird is a saving as it will provide more than one meal and it is so adaptable that there is never any problem with leftovers.

Chicken pieces are good for a quick meal. The most economical joints are the drumsticks and thighs – there is a lot of meat on them.

Frozen oven ready chickens are nearly always young birds that should never be overcooked, but you may occasionally come across a boiling fowl which is good value for money as there is plenty of meat on it and the flavour is good. These are old laying birds and are best slowly casseroled.

The rather bland taste of frozen chicken lends itself to the addition of other flavours. Most keen cooks like to make their own stuffings or at least add to the bought packet variety. For a change, flavour the bird with herb butter or bacon tucked under the skin of the breast before roasting – much simpler than making an elaborate stuffing. Or roast it the French way with the addition of a little stock in the tin.

Make a little chicken go a long way by stir frying. Two chicken breasts cut into fine strips and cooked this way, served with plenty of crispy vegetables, can be enough for six people.

CHICKEN GALANTINE

If you cannot get a boiling fowl, add a roasting bird halfway through the cooking of the hock and trotters.

| **2 pig's trotters, split** |
| **1 gammon hock** |
| **1 boiling fowl about 4 lb (1.8 kg)** |
| **Ground black pepper** |
| **2 bay leaves** |
| **A little mace** |
| **1 oz (25 g) gelatine** |
| **4 hard boiled eggs** |
| **Chopped parsley** |
| **Salt** |

Put the pig's trotters, hock and legs of the chicken in the base of a deep ovenproof casserole. Cover with water. Put the rest of the chicken on top, season with pepper, bay leaves and a little mace. Bring to the boil for a few minutes. Cover with a tight-fitting lid and cook in a slow oven 300 deg F, 150 deg C, gas mark 2, for 4 to 5 hours until really tender.

Lift out all the meat, leave until cool enough to handle, then discard all fat, skin and bone, and cut the meat in fairly big strips. Skim off all fat from the stock, taste and adjust seasoning. Strain into a measuring jug. If more than 1 pint (600 ml) return to the pan and reduce to 1 pint (600 ml). In the measuring jug, mix the powdered gelatine with 5 table-spoons of cold stock. Allow to set as a sponge, then add the measured boil-ing stock and stir well. Cool.

Take a 3 pint (1.7 lt) terrine, float a little of the cooled stock into the base of the terrine and sprinkle very generously with chopped parsley. Put in half the meat lengthways, adding a little seasoning and a little stock between the layers. Put the shelled hard boiled eggs end to end in a line and cover with the remainder of the strips of meat and enough stock to cover. Cover with a lid or piece of foil and chill for several hours until firm.

Chicken Galantine

To turn out, dip the terrine in boiling water for a moment, then turn out on to a dish. Decorate with fresh parsley and serve cut into fairly thick slices, with salad.

Serves 10 at least

CHINESE STIR FRY CHICKEN

You need just one large chicken breast to serve four people, it helps to have the breast slightly frozen before cutting into pencil thin strips.

| **1 large chicken breast, about 6 to 8 oz (175 g to 225 g)** |
| **12 oz (350 g) white cabbage** |
| **6 spring onions** |
| **2 level teaspoons cornflour** |
| **2 tablespoons sherry** |
| **2 tablespoons corn oil** |
| **Salt and pepper** |
| **1 red pepper, seeded and thinly sliced** |
| **12 oz (350 g) bean sprouts** |
| **¼ pint (150 ml) chicken stock** |
| **3 tablespoons soy sauce** |

Slice the chicken into fine pencil-thin strips about 2 inches (5 cm) long. Shred the cabbage very finely. Cut the spring onions into 2 inch (5 cm) lengths. Blend the cornflour with the sherry.

Heat the oil in a wok or large heavy saucepan until very hot. Season the chicken and add to the pan and cook over a fierce heat for a minute, stir-ring constantly, tossing and moving the chicken about the pan. Lift out with a slotted spoon and put on a plate.

Add the cabbage, red pepper, bean sprouts, spring onions to the pan and cook for 3 to 4 minutes, tossing con-stantly. Return the chicken to the pan and stir in the stock and soy sauce with the blended cornflour and cook for a minute until thickened and creamy and the vegetables are still crisp. Taste and adjust seasoning.

Serves 4 to 5

CHICKEN PUFF PIES

This uses up leftover chicken and ham and stretches it to a meal for 4. If you are short of cooked chicken and ham, spin it out with some sliced mushrooms.

| **About 6 oz (175 g) cooked chicken** |
| **About 6 oz (175 g) cooked ham** |
| **1 tablespoon chopped parsley** |
| **10.6 oz (300 g) can condensed mushroom soup** |
| **8 oz (227 g) packet bought puff pastry, thawed** |
| **Beaten egg or milk to glaze** |

Heat the oven to 425 deg F, 220 deg C, gas mark 7. Cut up the chicken and ham into small pieces and mix with the parsley and the can of con-densed mushroom soup. Roll out the pastry to 12 by 12 inches (30 by 30 cm). Cut in half and then half again, leaving four 6 inch (15 cm) squares.

Put ¼ of the mixture into the middle of each square. Dampen all the way round the edges of each square with water. Pick up the 4 corners of the first square and pinch them together in the middle, then pinch each of the 4 sides together evenly all the way to the corners. Repeat with the other 3 squares. Brush with beaten egg or milk and put on a baking tray and cook for about 15 minutes until well risen and evenly browned.

Serves 4

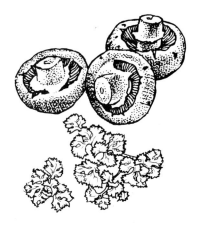

FRENCH ROAST CHICKEN WITH GARLIC AND HERB BUTTER

Cooking a chicken like this gives it a lovely flavour and keeps it moist.

3½lb (1.5 kg) roasting chicken
2 oz (50 g) butter
1 rounded tablespoon chopped mixed fresh herbs
1 clove garlic, crushed
Freshly ground black pepper
½ pint (300 ml) water
½ oz (12.5 g) cornflour
3 to 4 tablespoons white wine

Heat the oven to 350 deg F, 180 deg C, gas mark 4.

Wipe the chicken inside and out and remove the giblets. Cream the butter, herbs, garlic and pepper until soft and blended.

Put your hand under the skin on the breast of the chicken and work so that the skin is separated from the flesh. Take the creamed butter and spread over the breast and under the skin, working down over the leg joint. It is easiest to use your hand for this.

Place the chicken in a roasting tin with the giblets and water, cover and roast in the oven for 45 minutes, then remove the cover and turn the chicken to allow it to brown all over. First turn it on its side and then cook for a further 30 to 45 minutes turning, until tender.

The chicken is tender when the thickest part of the leg is pierced with a skewer and the juices run clear.

Place the cornflour in a saucepan and blend with the wine. Lift the chicken on to a serving dish and strain the juices into the saucepan, bring to the boil, stirring until thickened, then taste and adjust seasoning. Simmer for 2 minutes, and pour into a sauce boat and serve with the chicken.

Serves 6

Saturday Chicken

SATURDAY CHICKEN

So called because I often make this on Saturday before I go shopping. Into the oven it goes ready for lunch and if we are late it doesn't seem to matter. Any leftover wine or cider will do for this recipe.

6 chicken joints
Salt
Ground black pepper
14 oz (397 g) can peeled tomatoes
¼ pint (150 ml) boiling water
1 chicken stock cube
¼ pint (150 ml) wine or cider
2 tablespoons packet sage and onion stuffing mix
1 clove garlic, crushed
1 tablespoon redcurrant jelly
Chopped parsley

Heat the oven to 325 deg F, 160 deg C, gas mark 3

Pull the skins off the chicken joints and put them in a non-stick frying pan with the chicken joints and fry so that the fat runs out of the skins and the joints are brown on both sides. Lift out the chicken and place in an ovenproof casserole. Drain off any fat in the pan and save for another recipe.

Season the chicken well in the cas-

Roast Poussin with Garlic Potatoes

serole. Add all the remaining ingredients except the parsley to the pan and bring to the boil, stirring so that the stock cube dissolves. Pour over the chicken, cover and cook in the oven for about 1½ hours or until the chicken has become tender.

Taste and check seasoning and sprinkle with parsley and serve with plain boiled rice or pasta.

Serves 6

ROAST POUSSIN WITH GARLIC POTATOES

A special dish for a special occasion.

12 oz (350 g) peeled potatoes
White flour
Knob of butter
1 tablespoon oil
1 clove garlic, crushed
Salt
Ground black pepper
2 poussins

Heat the oven to 400 deg F, 200 deg C, gas mark 6.

Cut the potatoes into cubes the size of large sugar lumps. Put in a pan and cover with cold water, bring to the boil for one minute, then drain. Dust the potatoes with flour. Well grease a shallow dish about 8 inches (20 cm) across with the butter then add the oil and garlic and season well.

Lay the poussins on top of the potatoes and cover the breasts with pieces of buttered paper. Roast in the oven for 20 minutes then remove the paper and continue cooking for a further 25 to 30 minutes or until golden brown and the potatoes are tender.

Serves 2

EGGS
for easy cooking

Cooks love eggs and the wise cook is never without a good supply. Eggs are versatile, easy to use, easy to digest, and most people like them. They are always obtainable and their price remains reasonable. Store them in a cool place, larder or refrigerator, and there is always the basis of a quick, inexpensive meal ready to hand. If you keep them in the refrigerator, take them out and let them reach kitchen temperature before using. Beaten when warm rather than cold the whites produce far greater volume for meringues or soufflés.

Most people are now familiar with the grading system, from Grade 1 for the largest down to Grades 5 or 6 for the smallest.

Brown eggs or white? The answer is that it does not matter, the difference is only in the eye of the beholder. In America they pay extra for pure white ones, we do the same for dark brown.

They are all good.

Boil them, scramble them, fry them with bacon, make an omelette, make mayonnaise or meringues. The egg is the basis of most cakes and many sauces. It takes kindly to cheese and to vegetables of all kinds, and it can help you to achieve spectacular success with many simple dishes. Take the soufflé, for instance. A good soufflé, golden and well risen, puffing up in its dish as you take it out of the oven, does a lot for your reputation as a cook. Contrary to popular belief, there is no mystery about soufflés and it is truthfully said that if you can make a white sauce you can make a soufflé. The important thing is that it should be eaten straight out of the oven. There should not be too much trouble over this!

COTSWOLD SOUFFLÉ

Essential to serve at once as it begins to sink after a few moments.

2 oz (50 g) butter

1½ oz (40 g) plain flour

½ pint (300 ml) hot milk

Salt

Freshly ground black pepper

1 level teaspoon made mustard

5 oz (150 g) strong Cheddar cheese, grated

1 tablespoon chopped chives

4 large eggs

Butter a 2 pint (a good litre) or four ½ pint (300 ml) soufflé dishes. Heat the oven to 375 deg F, 190 deg C, gas mark 5 and place a baking sheet in it.

Melt the butter in a saucepan, stir in the flour and cook for 2 minutes without browning. Remove the pan from the heat and stir in the hot milk. Return to the heat and bring to the boil, stirring until it thickens, then add the seasoning and mustard and leave to cool. Stir in the cheese and chives.

Separate the eggs and beat the yolks one at a time into the cheese sauce. Whisk the egg whites with a rotary, hand or electric whisk until stiff, but not dry. Stir one heaped tablespoon into the cheese sauce and then carefully fold in the remainder.

Pour into the buttered soufflé dish or dishes and bake in the oven on the hot baking sheet for about 40 minutes for the large dish and 30 minutes for the individual dishes. Serve at once with basil tomato sauce.

Serves 4

Cotswold Soufflé

BASIL TOMATO SAUCE

A good basic tomato sauce that freezes well. Make when tomatoes are at their cheapest, or use a 14 oz (397 g) can of tomatoes.

1 oz (25 g) butter

1 large onion, chopped

1 fat clove of garlic, crushed

1 level tablespoon flour

1 lb (450 g) ripe tomatoes, skinned

½ pint (300 ml) stock

1 teaspoon caster sugar

Salt and ground black pepper to taste

1 level teaspoon chopped fresh basil

Melt the butter and gently fry the onion and garlic for about 5 minutes until soft. Add the flour and blend well. Stir in tomatoes, mash down a little, add the stock, sugar and seasoning. Bring to the boil, cover and simmer until everything is soft and tender, about 10 minutes. Sieve the sauce or reduce to a purée in a blender or processor. Rinse out the saucepan, return the tomato sauce to it with the basil and reheat. Taste and check seasoning.

Serves 4

FARMER'S OMELETTE

A substantial omelette to enjoy with crusty bread.

1 oz (25 g) butter

1 onion, chopped

4 oz (100 g) cooked potato, diced

2 oz (50 g) chopped ham

A little chopped parsley

4 eggs

4 tablespoons cold water

Salt and pepper

Melt the butter in a large non-stick frying pan, add the onion and cook slowly for about 5 minutes until soft, then add the potatoes and ham and heat through. Sprinkle over the parsley.

Heat the grill to moderate. Beat the eggs, water and seasoning together with a fork. Pour into the pan and cook, drawing the egg from the sides of the pan to the centre so that the egg runs through to cook on the base of the pan. Put under the grill to set the top and then slide the omelette on to a plate.

Serves 2

EGG MOUSSE

Serve either as a first course or for lunch. I sometimes add chopped chives if I have plenty.

¾ oz (19 g) gelatine

6 tablespoons water

10½ oz (298 g) can condensed consommé

8 hard boiled eggs

½ pint (300 ml) double cream

½ pint (300 ml) mayonnaise (see page 54)

Salt and pepper

A little chopped parsley

Place the gelatine in a bowl with the water and leave to stand for 3 minutes then place over a bowl of gently simmering water until dissolved. Remove from the heat and stir in the undiluted consommé.

Chop the eggs. Whisk the cream in a large bowl until thick and then stir in the mayonnaise and eggs, mix well and finally blend in three quarters of the consommé. Taste and check seasoning and turn into a 2½ pint (1.4 lt) serving dish. Leave in a cool place to set.

Stir the chopped parsley into the remaining consommé and pour over the set mousse, return to the refrigerator until the top is set.

Serves 8

Mayonnaise

MAYONNAISE

This method makes mayonnaise so simple. For a variation you can add a few chopped fresh herbs or a good pinch of curry powder.

2 eggs
1 level teaspoon salt
Plenty of ground black pepper
Scant teaspoon made mustard
1 teaspoon caster sugar
1 tablespoon wine or cider vinegar
1 pint (600 ml) corn oil
Juice of one lemon

Place all the ingredients except the oil and lemon juice in a processor or blender and process for a few moments, then add the oil in a slow steady stream until all has been added. The mayonnaise will now be thick. Add the lemon juice and process again. Taste and check seasoning.

Store in a screw topped container in the refrigerator for up to one month.

Makes about one pint (600 ml) mayonnaise.

LEMON HOLLANDAISE

Hollandaise is a wonderful sauce made with egg yolks and butter. It enhances trout, salmon, artichokes, asparagus and other vegetables.

3 egg yolks
4 teaspoons lemon juice
4 oz (100 g) unsalted butter
¼ teaspoon salt
Pinch of white pepper

Put the egg yolks in a blender or processor with the lemon juice and blend on maximum speed for a few seconds.

Just before serving, bring the butter to the boil in a small saucepan. Switch the blender or processor to maximum speed for a few seconds and slowly pour on the boiling butter, blend until thick, add the seasoning and pour the sauce into a warmed sauceboat. Serve at once.

Serves 4

Lemon and Lime Curd

MERINGUES

Remember to use egg whites at room temperature and follow the method exactly. Use caster sugar for white, creamy coloured meringues and soft brown sugar for darker more squidgy ones.

4 egg whites

8 oz (225 g) caster sugar

Whipping cream

Heat the oven to 200 deg F, 100 deg C, gas mark ¼. Line two baking sheets with silicone paper.

Place the egg whites in a large bowl and whisk on high speed with an electric or hand rotary whisk until they form soft peaks. Add the sugar a teaspoon at a time, whisking well after each addition, until all the sugar has been added. Using two dessert-spoons, spoon the meringue out on to the baking sheets, putting twelve meringues on each tray.

Bake in the oven for 3 to 4 hours, until the meringues are firm and dry and will lift easily from the silicone paper. They will be a very pale off white or slightly darker if you have used soft brown sugar.

Whisk the cream until thick and use to sandwich the meringue shells together.

Makes 12 double meringues

LEMON AND LIME CURD

You can just put everything into the top of a double boiler – stir from time to time and strain when thick enough to coat the back of the spoon – but this method takes twice as long.

3 lemons

2 limes

8 oz (225 g) butter

1 lb (450 g) caster sugar

5 large eggs

Peel 1 lemon and both limes very thinly, taking off only the outside zest. Squeeze out juice from all fruits. Put in a pan with the butter and caster sugar. Heat slowly at first until the sugar has dissolved and the mixture is just below simmering.

Break eggs into a bowl, beat together to blend well but not to be frothy. Gently beat in the butter mixture from the pan. Strain into a bowl, stand bowl over a pan of simmering water, stir until the mixture thickens enough to coat the back of a spoon, about 20 minutes. Pour into about 3 clean jam jars, place a wax disc on top. When cold, cover with a lid or a cling film top. Store in the refrigerator for up to 6 weeks.

Yield about 3 lb (1.3 kg)

CHRISTMAS FAVOURITES

Christmas is the traditional festival. Most families
celebrate it strictly according to the rules of their
time-honoured customs. The tree goes in a certain
corner, to be covered with the decorations that have
been carefully preserved over the years. The same
games are played that were played last year, the same
jokes are told. What we eat is no exception to this rule
– after all, there is nothing more traditional than
turkey, Christmas pudding and mince pies, and you
depart from those at your peril.
This programme has acquired Christmas traditions
of its own. Here are some of our favourites that
regular viewers will remember over the past ten years.
We make no apology for presenting them again.
There is one newcomer, Gleneagles pâté. Briefly, it
consists of three different pâtés, trout, taramasalata or
smoked salmon, and mackerel, sandwiched together.
Chilled and sliced, its contrasting colours look like
Neapolitan ice cream and served with brown toast or
hot French bread it makes a marvellous party dish for
any time of the year. But we hope that it may become
part of *your* Christmas tradition.
It remains only to recommend to you our recipe
for liqueur whisky – and to wish you a very
Merry Christmas.

GLENEAGLES PÂTÉ

Three smoked fish pâtés.

A spectacular looking fish pâté for a party, especially easy if you have a food processor. I lined the pâté or loaf tin with cling film then very thin slices of smoked salmon. This is a luxury, there is no real need to do it. You could turn the pâté out and scatter it with chopped fresh parsley. You get the spectacular effect when you slice the pâté, and reveal the Neapolitan stripes.

As an alternative to smoked cod's roe, use 8 oz (225 g) smoked salmon pieces and no tomato purée.

This pâté freezes well for up to one month.

4 oz (100 g) vacuum pack sliced smoked salmon

Trout pâté

14 oz (400 g) smoked trout, large fish skinned and boned
6 oz (175 g) butter, melted
4 oz (100 g) rich cream cheese
Juice of half a lemon
Ground black pepper

Taramasalata pâté

8 oz (225 g) smoked cod's roe, skinned, or 8 oz jar or tin
5 oz (150 g) butter, melted
4 oz (100 g) rich cream cheese
2 tablespoons tomato purée
Juice of half a lemon
Ground black pepper

Mackerel pâté

12 oz (350 g) smoked mackerel, skinned
6 oz (175 g) butter, melted
4 oz (100 g) rich cream cheese
Juice of a lemon
Ground black pepper

You will need a 2½ pint (1.4 lt) loaf tin or pâté dish.

First line pâté dish or loaf tin with cling film, then the thinly sliced smoked salmon. Weigh out each pâté separately. Put all ingredients for the trout pâté in a blender or processor and mix to a smooth pâté. If using a blender it helps to do this in two batches. Taste and check seasoning, it may need a little salt. Spread this pâté on the base of the dish or tin in a thin layer, put in the refrigerator to firm up.

Next make the taramasalata pâté in the same way – no need to wash up the blender or processor in between. Taste. The tomato purée will make the pâté a bright pink, which is a lovely contrast as the middle layer. Take the pâté from the fridge and spread the taramasalata pink pâté on top. Return to the fridge.

Last, make the mackerel pâté in the same way and spread over the pink pâté. Fold any spare cling film over the top. Chill overnight. Next day, turn out and decorate with parsley or watercress and serve cut in thick slices with hot melba toast and butter.

Serves 14 at least as a first course

LEMON AND THYME STUFFING

1 oz (25 g) butter
1 onion, chopped
1 lb (450 g) pork sausagemeat
4 oz (100 g) fresh white breadcrumbs
Grated rind and juice of one lemon
1 level teaspoon salt
Ground black pepper
2 tablespoons chopped parsley
1 level teaspoon fresh thyme, chopped or 1 level teaspoon dried thyme

Melt the butter in a saucepan, add the onion and fry gently until soft, about 10 minutes. Stir in the remaining ingredients and mix well together.

Use to stuff a 14 to 16 lb (6.3 to 7.2 kg) turkey.

CHESTNUT STUFFING

If you cannot get dried chestnuts, use a 1 lb 15 oz (880 g) can of whole chestnuts in water, or fresh chestnuts.

8 oz (225 g) dried chestnuts, soaked overnight in cold water
8 oz (225 g) streaky bacon, chopped
2 oz (50 g) butter
4 oz (100 g) fresh breadcrumbs
1 egg, beaten
1 bunch watercress, finely chopped
1 tablespoon caster sugar
2 teaspoons salt
Ground black pepper

Drain the liquid from the chestnuts and chop coarsely.

Fry the bacon slowly to allow the fat to run out, add chestnuts and then increase the heat and fry quickly until bacon is crisp, and nuts beginning to colour. Lift out with a slotted spoon and put in a bowl. Add the butter to the pan with the bacon fat and allow to melt, then add the breadcrumbs and fry until brown, turn into the bowl. Add the remaining ingredients and mix well. Use to stuff the body cavity of a 14 to 16 lb (6.3 to 7.2 kg) turkey.

Gleneagles Pâté. The pâté shown here is made from smoked salmon pieces in place of smoked cod's roe.

ROAST TURKEY

Thaw the turkey if frozen. Check the weight of the bird with stuffing and calculate the cooking time. Heat the oven.

Put a large piece of foil in the roasting tin. Lift the turkey on to it and season well. Wrap foil over the bird loosely with the fold at the top. Place the turkey on a shelf just below the middle of the oven.

To brown the turkey undo the foil and rub the breast and legs with butter. Cook with the foil open for the last 1¼ hours of the cooking time for a large bird and about 50 minutes for a small bird.

The turkey is cooked if the thickest part is pierced with a skewer and the juices run out clear, test in the leg. After cooking, cover the turkey with foil and keep warm in the oven and allow to rest for 10 minutes before carving.

ROASTING TIMES

5 lb (2.3 kg) 350 deg F, 180 deg C, gas mark 4, 2 hours 30 minutes.
10 lb (4.5 kg) 350 deg F, 180 deg C, gas mark 4, 3 hours 15 minutes.
15 lb (6.8 kg) 350 deg F, 180 deg C, gas mark 4, 4 hours.
20 lb (9 kg) 325 deg F, 160 deg C, gas mark 3, 5 hours.

BREAD SAUCE

1 onion, peeled

3 cloves

¾ pint (425 ml) milk

3 oz (75 g) fresh white breadcrumbs

Salt and pepper

A knob of butter

Take the onion and stick the cloves into it, place in a saucepan with the milk. Bring slowly to the boil and then turn off the heat and leave the milk to infuse for 30 minutes.

Lift out the onion and stir in the breadcrumbs, seasoning and butter. Reheat to almost boiling point, remove from the heat. Cover with a piece of damp greaseproof paper and keep warm until required.

CHIPOLATA SAUSAGES

Grill the sausages, pricking them if liked, under a medium grill for about 10 to 15 minutes. Turn regularly so that they are evenly browned. If you like little sausages, give each chipolata an extra twist in the centre to make it half the size, then cut apart.

BACON ROLLS

Take the rind off streaky bacon rashers and stretch on a wooden board with the back of a knife so that they are twice the original length. Cut each rasher in half and roll up. Place on long skewers and grill for 6 to 8 minutes under a moderate grill turning once so that they are golden brown.

ROAST POTATOES

Roast for 1½ to 1¾ hours above the turkey. They take longer than usual as the oven temperature is lower. If oven space is short you could do these in an electric frying pan or even a deep fat fryer.

FRESH CRANBERRY SAUCE

8 oz (225 g) cranberries

10 oz (275 g) caster sugar

1 whole thin-skinned orange, quartered and pips removed

Place all the ingredients in a blender or food processor and purée to a chunky mince consistency. Turn into a small bowl and serve.

Roast Turkey with trimmings

Christmas Pudding

CHRISTMAS PUDDING

When the pudding is cooked, cool and then cover with a new piece of foil. Store in a cool place until Christmas day, then boil for a further 3 hours.

2 oz (50 g) self-raising flour
Good pinch mixed spice
Good pinch grated nutmeg
4 oz (100 g) currants
4 oz (100 g) sultanas
4 oz (100 g) stoned raisins
3 oz (75 g) fresh white breadcrumbs
3 oz (75 g) shredded suet
1 oz (25 g) chopped mixed peel

1 oz (25 g) almonds, blanched
1 small cooking apple
1 rounded tablespoon marmalade
3 oz (75 g) grated carrot
4 oz (100 g) soft brown sugar
2 eggs, beaten

Grease a 1½ pint (900 ml) pudding basin.

Sift together the flour and spices. Put the currants and sultanas in a large bowl and roughly chop the raisins and add with the breadcrumbs, suet and peel. Roughly chop the almonds. Peel the apple and coarsely grate, add to the bowl with the almonds, marmalade and carrot. Stir in the spiced flour and sugar. Mix well and then stir in the eggs.

Turn into the greased basin, cover the top with greaseproof paper and a foil lid. Simmer gently for 6 hours. Lift out of the pan, leaving the greaseproof paper and foil in place and cool.

When cold re-cover and store in a cool place until required.

Serves 8

MINCE PIE

One large pie means that you have lots of filling. Use a hard margarine for the pastry. Serve with brandy butter or cream.

Pastry

8 oz (225 g) strong plain flour
½ teaspoon salt
6 oz (175 g) hard margarine
About 9 tablespoons, or a scant ¼ pint (150 ml) cold water

Filling

1 lb (450 g) jar mincemeat
Milk
Caster sugar

For the pastry: sift the flour and salt into a mixing bowl. Coarsely grate the margarine into the bowl. Stir in just sufficient water to make a firm dough and then roll out on a lightly floured surface to make a strip about ½ inch (1.25 cm) thick and 6 inches (15 cm) wide. Fold the pastry in three and give it a quarter turn to the left. Roll out again into a strip and fold into three. Wrap the pastry in foil and chill in the refrigerator for 30 minutes. Heat the oven to 425 deg F, 220 deg C, gas mark 7.

Divide the pastry into 2 portions, one slightly larger than the other. Roll out smaller portion to a circle about ¼ inch (5 mm) thick and use to line a 10 inch (25 cm) pie plate made of enamel, tin or foil. Spoon in the mincemeat.

Roll out the remaining pastry to a circle ¼ inch (5 mm) thick. Brush with milk at the edges of the pie and cover the mincemeat with the second pastry circle. Press edges firmly together to seal, trim off any excess pastry and crimp edges to make a decorative finish. Chill for 10 minutes.

Brush the top of the pie with milk and bake in the oven for 25 minutes until the pastry is golden brown. Sprinkle with caster sugar and serve warm.

Serves 8

BRANDY CREAM

Try this for a change as a lighter accompaniment to mince pies and Christmas pudding.

¼ pint (150 ml) double cream
1 tablespoon caster sugar
2 tablespoons brandy

Put all the ingredients in a bowl and whisk until thick and the mixture forms soft peaks. Pile in a dish and serve chilled.

BRANDY BUTTER

Store any left over in the freezer for about 3 months.

8 oz (225 g) unsalted butter
8 oz (225 g) icing sugar, sieved
6 tablespoons brandy

Cream the butter with a wooden spoon until soft. Then gradually beat in the icing sugar and continue beating until the mixture is light and fluffy, then beat in the brandy.

Turn the butter into a serving dish and chill in the refrigerator to harden before serving. If made in advance, leave the butter at room temperature for about 30 minutes before serving.

LIGHTLY FRUITED CAKE WITH PINEAPPLE

This is a moist, less rich Christmas cake. Best made just before Christmas and kept in the refrigerator.

2 oz (50 g) glacé cherries
7 oz (200 g) self-raising flour
8 oz (225 g) can pineapple in chunks, rings or crushed, excluding the juice
5 oz (150 g) butter
4½ oz (112 g) soft brown sugar
2 large eggs, beaten
2 tablespoons milk
12 oz (350 g) mixed dried fruit

Grease an 8 inch (20 cm) round cake tin and line with greased greaseproof paper. Cut the cherries in halves and roll in flour. Drain the pineapple and chop finely.

Cream the butter and sugar in a mixing bowl. Beat in the eggs, adding a tablespoon of flour with the last amount of egg. Fold in the flour, milk and last of all the fruit, including the pineapple.

Turn into the prepared tin and place in the oven at 325 deg F, 160 deg C, gas mark 3 for about 2 hours until the cake is a pale golden brown and shrinking from the sides of the tin. Leave to cool in the tin, remove the paper and store in a plastic container in the refrigerator.

LIQUEUR WHISKY

Tim Jones, who was director of the Thames TV *A Plus* Christmas food programme last year gave me this easy recipe. Sadly you have to start with a bottle of whisky, but it is splendidly smooth and mature tasting. Honeysmoke essence can be bought from home brew wine and beer shops.

1 pint (600 ml) whisky
8 oz (225 g) caster sugar
3 teaspoons glycerine
2 or 3 drops of tincture of capsicum
10 drops honeysmoke essence

Place the measured whisky into an empty bottle, add sugar, glycerine, tincture of capsicum and honeysmoke essence. Put on the lid and shake really well to dissolve the sugar. Leave overnight and it is ready to drink the next day.

INDEX